WORLD ISSUES

TERRORISM

LIGHTS, CAMERA, WAR

A look at the way the world is today

Helen Donohoe

Franklin Watts
London • Sydney

ABOUT THIS BOOK

TERRORISM looks at all aspects of this important and varied subject. This book will help you to understand the issues behind terrorist acts. You will learn more about the effects of terrorism on our global community and how terrorism affects the stability of our everyday lives.

   You will find information on many aspects of terrorism – from the definition and causes of terrorism, to the fight against terrorists and attempts around the world to create a safer world for all.

New updated edition printed in 2006
© Aladdin Books Ltd 2006
Produced by Aladdin Books Ltd
2&3 Fitzroy Mews
London W1T 6DF

ISBN 978–07496–7325–3 (Hardcover)
ISBN 978–07496–7289–8 (Paperback)

Original edition first published in 2004 by

Franklin Watts	Franklin Watts Australia
338 Euston Road	Hachette Children's Books
London	Level 17/207 Kent Street
NW1 3BH	Sydney NSW 2000

Designers: Flick, Book Design and Graphics
Pete Bennett – PBD
Editor: Katie Harker
Editorial consultant: Professor Stuart Croft, Department of Political Science and International Studies, University of Birmingham, UK.

The author, Helen Donohoe, has an MA in politics and writes for a wide audience, including senior politicians and journalists.

Printed in Malaysia   All rights reserved
A CIP catalogue record for this book is available from the British Library.
Dewey Classification: 303.6'25

CONTENTS

INTRODUCTION

It seems that terrorism is never far from our lives. Stories of terrorist acts, both past and present, are constantly in the news. And today, with the arrival of new global threats and more sinister terrorist methods, we are analysing, more than ever before, why terrorism occurs, the effects it has and how it can be prevented.

Terrorism impacts on many lives, and the passion and anger felt by the communities affected never goes away. For this reason, terrorism will always be a feature of the news. The trials of the Lockerbie bombers of 1988, the Omagh bombers of 1998 and more recently the 'shoe bomber' in the USA received as much media attention as the terrorist atrocities themselves.

The aftermath of the Omagh bomb in 1998. Both Catholics and Protestants were among the victims.

Lockerbie, Scotland – 1988.

• On 21 December 1988, a Pan Am Boeing 747 jet, flying from London to New York, exploded and crashed down on the Scottish town of Lockerbie. All 259 passengers were killed along with 11 people on the ground.
• In 2001, Abdel Baset Al Megrahi, a Libyan intelligence agent, was found guilty of the bombing. It is believed that he had acted in revenge for the 1986 bombing of Tripoli, Libya, by US warplanes flying from British bases.

Omagh, County Tyrone, Northern Ireland – 1998.

• On 15 August 1998, a bomb exploded in a busy shopping street in Omagh, Northern Ireland. The blast killed 29 people and injured at least 220.
• No one claimed responsibility for the bombing but the atrocity was linked to a group called the 'Real IRA'. In August 2003, Michael McKevitt was found guilty of directing the activities of the Real IRA and sentenced to 20 years in prison.

The terrorist atrocities carried out in the US on 11 September 2001, when over 3,000 lives were lost, brought home the devastation of terrorism to people across the globe, on a scale that has never been witnessed before. Yet, terrorism is not a new phenomenon. Throughout history, individuals, groups, governments and rebel organisations have all used terror to achieve their goals. Terrorist atrocities have been largely driven by differences of religious and spiritual beliefs, or territorial, political and moral ideals. As the modern world develops, the threat of violence is something that we will continually have to face, challenge, reassess and learn how to deal with.

Terrorism in 17th century England

- In 1604, a group of English Catholics began planning a coup. They were protesting against their King, James I, who was persecuting Catholics.
- The group conspired to blow up the House of Lords on 5 November 1605, the day that Parliament assembled, in an attempt to kill the King.
- Guido (Guy) Fawkes, who had fought for Spain as a hired soldier, was to set the fuse and flee to Spain. Meanwhile, Robert Catesby, the leader of the plot, was to raise a rebellion among Catholics in northern England.
- The plan was betrayed and on 4 November 1605, Guy Fawkes was found in a cellar below the House of Lords, with large quantities of gunpowder. Catesby failed to start a rebellion in the north and he later died attempting to do so.
- In January 1606, Guy Fawkes and the other surviving plotters were executed as traitors.
- Despite the rebellion, Catholic repression continued across the country.

Workers continued to search the rubble of the World Trade Center for 230 days after the September 11th attacks.

A HISTORY OF TERRORISM

The world has faced the threat of terrorism throughout its history. Whether we talk about the gunpowder plot of 1605, when Guy Fawkes tried to destroy the English Parliament, or the modern day threats of Islamic fundamentalists – terrorism is the unfortunate result of different citizens, with opposite views, living side by side. Terrorist acts are committed by different types of people, in the name of many different causes. The nature of terrorism is also changing, since terrorists increasingly use different methods to achieve their goals. To counteract the threat of terrorism, countries are adopting more stringent and sometimes controversial measures, to protect their boundaries and to keep their citizens safe.

WHAT IS TERRORISM?

Broadly speaking, terrorism is the use of violence or intimidation to achieve a desired end. A terrorist might use these methods to influence a government, or to attempt to change the behaviour of a group of citizens. An extreme act involving widespread devastation, like that of 11 September 2001, stands out as a clear example of terrorism at its worst. But terrorism can also include threats and intimidation. The term terrorism is also very broad. It can include the systematical killing of people in Iraq by various groups as well as the attacks and kidnappings by Hezbollah in Israel and South Lebanon in 2006.

The twin towers of the World Trade Center, as they once stood.

On 11 September 2001, two hijacked planes crashed into the World Trade Center. Within two hours the twin towers had collapsed.

MEANING OF TERRORISM

The first recorded use of the term 'terrorism' was in 1795, in reference to the French government's *Reign of Terror* – a period that saw the execution of many presumed enemies of the state. The Jacobians, who led the government at the time, were revolutionaries and gradually the term 'terrorism' was used to describe violent revolutionary activity in general. But the use of 'terrorist' in an anti-government sense was not until the late 19th century, with reference to revolutionary movements in Ireland and Russia.

The first official attempt to define terrorism in modern times was in the 1960s, when the United Nations agreed that terrorist activities needed to be acknowledged by the rule of law. However, very few countries have since defined terrorism in their domestic litigation. The UK's Terrorism Act 2000 defines terrorism as 'the use or threat of action to influence a government or intimidate the public for political, religious or ideological reasons'. Some examples might be murder, kidnapping or seizing public transport. The Terrorism Act 2006 includes new offences and amends existing ones.

11 September 2001 also brought devastation in Washington DC when a hijacked plane crashed into the Pentagon. All 64 passengers and 125 people inside the Pentagon lost their lives.

A difference of opinion

It is often said that one person's terrorist is another person's freedom fighter – somebody who uses violence to overthrow an undemocratic government may be seen as a terrorist or a liberator. Political judgements on what is legitimate and illegitimate killing can vary greatly. Yet, the key point about terrorism, on which almost everyone agrees, is that it is motivated by religious, social or political movements. This is what distinguishes terrorist activities from, say, murder or football hooliganism.

Politics in action

Some argue that terrorism is defined by the fact that it is used to terrorise the public (or a particular section of it) through threats or actual violence.

At times, it is difficult to separate the work of political activists and terrorists, as in the case of Northern Ireland, where some political parties share similar views to terrorist groups. Some also feel that this definition of terrorism describes the actions of countries too.

11 September 2001

• On the morning of 11 September 2001, four domestic flights within the United States were hijacked shortly after take-off.
• Two of the planes were diverted to New York and later crashed into the North and South towers of the World Trade Center. The towers collapsed within two hours.
• The third plane crashed into the Pentagon in Washington DC and a large section of the building collapsed.
• The fourth plane crashed into woodland in Pennsylvania after passengers confronted the hijackers.
• In total, over 3,000 lives were lost.

7

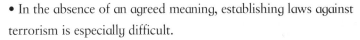

The UK Terrorism Act 2000

(amended and extended in The Terrorism Act 2006)
• In the absence of an agreed meaning, establishing laws against terrorism is especially difficult.
• The latest UK anti-terrorism law avoids this problem by listing 21 international terrorist organisations by name. Membership of these groups is illegal in the UK.
• There are six Islamic groups, four anti-Israel groups, eight separatist groups and three opposition groups.
• The list includes Hezbollah, which though armed, is a legal political party in the Middle Eastern country of Lebanon.
• Among the separatist groups, the Kurdistan Workers Party – active in Turkey – is illegal in the UK. However, the Kurdistan Democratic Party and the Patriotic Union of Kurdistan – Kurdish organisations active in Iraq – are legal in the UK.
• Among opposition groups, the Iranian People's Mujahideen is named, but not its Iraqi equivalent, the Iraqi National Congress.

Politics in action (continued)

Acts of terrorism often involve death and devastation and many would argue that this is also a common theme of 'war'.

For others, the civilian losses caused by the heavy bombing by Israel on Lebanon in 2006 are not far from acts of terrorism. Likewise, some consider the use of depleted uranium (DU) shells by British and American coalition forces in the 1991 Gulf War and the 2003 invasion of Iraq as terrorist behaviour – DU contaminates land and can cause illnesses such as cancer in civilians. These examples illustrate the complexity of defining terrorism in the modern world.

Can governments support terrorists too?

Terrorism is commonly directed at the actions of governments, but governments are not entirely blameless of supporting terrorist activities themselves.

In 2003, the USA accused Iran, Iraq, Sudan, Syria, Libya, North Korea and Cuba of supporting terrorism with financial and military resources. However, despite currently leading the 'war on terrorism', and opposing countries who they believe to hold weapons of mass destruction, the US and Britain also have a history of supporting terrorism. In 1979, when Russia invaded Afghanistan, the US gave financial, military and intelligence support to the 'Mujahideen', a coalition of resistance fighters who opposed the communist invasion of the region. When the Soviet army left in 1989, the US swiftly withdrew their support to the Mujahideen – an action that many believe has added to resentment of the US government by Islamic groups in Pakistan and Afghanistan. Ironically, Osama bin Laden, and other top officials from today's Islamic movements, were amongst the Mujahideen. He, and many of his fellow fighters, have since formed the al-Qaeda network and turned against their former American supporters.

Britain, too, has a history of supporting terrorist activity in order to protect its own interest. In 1918, the British government sent an army of ex-soldiers to British occupied Ireland in an attempt to control the 'rebel' population. The soldiers, known as Black and Tans, terrorised local communities by ransacking homes and setting fire to churches. The most infamous attack on the public came in November 1920 at Croke Park, Dublin, when soldiers opened fire on the crowd and killed twelve people.

But, like individuals, governments can also have a change of heart. In December 2003, the Libyan leader, Colonel Gaddafi, announced that his country would abandon its support for terrorists. Libya had long been on America's list of countries that sponsor terrorism.

THE CAUSES OF TERRORISM

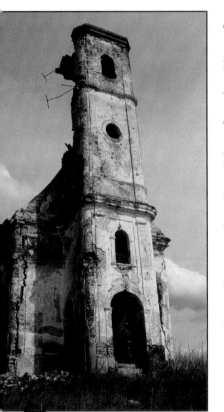

Religion was a major factor in terror atrocities in the former Yugoslavia during the 1990s.

Israelis and Palestinians are fighting about religious and territorial issues.

There is no single cause of terrorism. In most cases, terrorism is fuelled by very strong feelings of injustice, and a belief that there are no alternative ways to rectify the situation. Terrorists seek conflict in an attempt to change the way that life is currently organised on a local, national or global scale. In today's world, common causes of terrorism include feelings of discrimination over different cultural or religious beliefs, disputes over land or territory, feelings of political or economic inequality and feelings of moral or social injustice. These issues are widespread around the world.

RELIGIOUS TERRORISM –

Jewish Israelis and Muslim Palestinians

There has been a conflict between Arab Muslims and Jews throughout history. In bibilical times, Jewish people lived on the land that is now known as Israel. But in 800 AD, this area came under Arab rule and many Jews were forced to leave. For centuries, Jewish people still regarded this area to be their 'homeland', and in the early 20th century thousands started to move back there.

The conflict was intensified with the establishment of Israel and Palestine in 1948. After the Second World War,

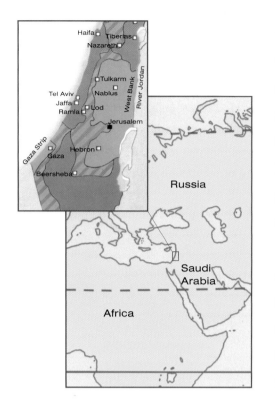

when millions of Jews were massacred by the Nazi regime, there was worldwide support for the creation of a country where Jews could live. The United Nations (UN) voted to divide Palestine into two states: Palestine (Arab) and Israel (Jewish). The Jews accepted the plan and declared independence for Israel in May 1948. However, the Arabs rejected the idea, claiming that, as the majority group, they were entitled to more land. As a result of the division over 700,000 Palestinians were forced to leave their homes.

This is just one of many events in history that sowed the seeds of anger and resentment amongst Israelis and Palestinians, leading to the terrorist atrocities of today. The main areas of land that are currently being disputed are known as the West Bank and the Gaza Strip. Although mostly Palestinians live there, the Israelis are seeking full control over the land. Neither side can agree on who should occupy the land and who should control it.

Buses have become a regular target for suicide bombers in Israel.

Conflict in Israel

• An international peace process began in 1993 in an attempt to resolve the conflict between Palestinians and Israelis.

• The momentum towards peace was interrupted in 1995 when Israeli Prime Minister Yitzhak Rabin was assassinated by a Jewish religious extremist.

• Conflict returned in 1996 with a series of devastating suicide bombings in Israel carried out by Islamic militant groups such as Hamas and Palestine Islamic Jihad.

• The terrorist atrocities continue to this day:

August 2003 – 23 killed and over 130 wounded in the suicide bombing of a bus in Jerusalem.

October 2003 – 21 people killed and 60 wounded by a female suicide bomber in a restaurant in Haifa.

July /August 2006 – Hezbollah kidnapping of Israeli soldiers led to Israeli bombings and military invasion of South Lebanon. Fragile ceasefire agreed; Israelis withdrew.

TERRITORIAL TERRORISM – Chechnya

The Chechen people largely originate from a Muslim population. For centuries, they lived in the mountainous Caucasus region of Russia, but they consistently resisted Soviet control.

During World War II, the Soviet dictator, Josef Stalin, accused the Chechens of co-operating with the Nazis. He forcibly deported the entire population to the Central Asian republic of Kazakhstan. Tens of thousands of Chechens died, and the survivors were only allowed to return home after Stalin's death in 1953.

Chechen freedom fighters

• In October 2002, Chechen terrorists stormed a theatre in Moscow and took 800 people hostage. Russian special troops stormed the theatre but the gas they used to disable the terrorists killed more than 120 hostages as well as some of the terrorists.
• In December 2002, suicide bombers attacked the headquarters of Chechnya's Russian-backed government in Grozny, killing 83 people.
• In September 2004, in Berlan, Russia, 331 children and teachers were killed in their school by Chechen Islamic terrorists.
• These, and similar attacks have been blamed on Chechen rebels, who are seeking political independence.

An ongoing conflict

In 1991, Chechnya declared itself independent from Russia. Three years later, the president of Russia at the time, Boris Yeltsin, sent Russian troops to take back control in Chechnya. A war ensued which lasted until 1996, when Chechnya became partly independent from Russia. About 80,000 people died in the struggle.

Seeking full independence

Now Chechens are seeking full independence and wish to be able to run their own country. This ongoing conflict has led to an uprising of Chechen rebel terrorists, with increasing terrorist activity. Terrorists have killed hundreds of citizens through bombings, and in particular, suicide bombings.

11

Chechen rebels (left) have been linked to many terrorist atrocities in Russia since the 1990s.

In 1999, the Russian Prime Minister, Vladimir Putin, sent troops into Chechnya again. There had been a spate of bombings on flats in Russia's capital, Moscow, and Putin blamed Chechen rebels. Since that time, many Chechens have fled their homeland, continued fighting has cost many lives, and poverty and violence is widespread.

Chechnya and al-Qaeda

It is now believed that Chechen rebels are supported by al-Qaeda. Many Muslim volunteers have gone to Chechnya to join the fight, reportedly after attending training camps linked with al-Qaeda, in Afghanistan or Pakistan. Chechen rebels also reportedly fought alongside al-Qaeda and Taliban forces against the US-led invasion of Afghanistan in 2001. The former Taliban regime was one of the only governments to recognise Chechen independence.

Chechnya facts

- Chechnya is a Republic within the Russian Federation with around one million citizens.
- The population of Chechnya is predominantly Muslim and this brings about conflict with the largely secular or Christian Russia.
- Chechens want independence from Russia, but the Russian government considers the area vital to maintaining its influence in the Caucasus region.

A member of the Northern Alliance continues in his hunt for al-Qaeda suspects during the US-led invasion of Afghanistan in 2001. It is believed that many Chechen rebels fought alongside the al-Qaeda and Taliban forces, having attended training camps in Afghanistan and Pakistan.

POLITICAL TERRORISM – Oklahoma, USA

Political terrorism is based upon a belief in different political ideologies. This type of terrorism is usually carried out by right or left wing extremists who despise a different political system.

On 19 April 1995, a bomb ripped the front from a nine-storey building in Oklahoma, USA, killing 168 people.

13

Before the events of 11 September 2001, the Oklahoma bomb in April 1995 was the biggest single act of terrorism on US soil. The atrocity killed 168 people, including 19 children, and injured more than 500. Timothy McVeigh was later convicted of the attack and executed in 2001.

McVeigh's politics

Timothy McVeigh was born in 1968 and grew up in a conservative rural community in New York State. He began collecting guns while still at school and after leaving school he became fascinated by right wing, racist and military focused literature. McVeigh

then became interested in what is known as the 'militia movement'. Like other followers, he believed that ordinary Americans were under imminent threat of attack, from nuclear war, communists or the central government.

Distrust of the government

Several events in the US fuelled McVeigh's belief that the central government interfered too much in people's lives. He was distressed by the Ruby Ridge catastrophe in 1992 when a siege and shootout by police killed the wife of racist Randy Weaver and their 14-year-old son.

The Weaver family had moved to a remote area in Northern Idaho, USA, to escape what they believed was a sinful world. Randy and his three other children survived.

It seems the final straw for McVeigh came in 1993, when David Koresh, the leader of a religious cult, died alongside more than 80 of his followers in a fire during an FBI assault on their compound in Waco, Texas. The government thought that Koresh was a gun-hoarding criminal who physically and sexually abused the several children he fathered with his followers, the 'Branch Davidians'. The police surrounded the home of the cult and ended a 51-day siege by storming the compound.

Nobody can be really sure what drove Timothy McVeigh to set off a bomb in Oklahoma City on that fateful day in 1995. However, the bombing was a pivotal event in American history. It changed the way that Americans looked at terrorism. In the hours after the Oklahoma bombing, fingers pointed to Middle Eastern organisations. Yet, the actual cause of the bombing meant that Americans had to come to terms with a terrorist threat that was very real within their own country.

14

It took six weeks for rescuers to find the victims of the Oklahoma bombing.

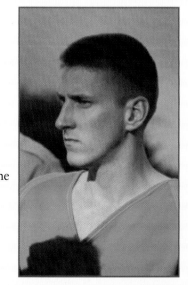

Timothy McVeigh and the Oklahoma bomb – key dates.

- 1968 – Timothy McVeigh born, Pendleton, New York.
- 1992 – Police forces storm the isolated home of white separatist Randy Weaver at Ruby Ridge, Idaho, the target of a guns investigation. His wife Vicki and their son, Sammy, are killed. The deaths raise questions about the excessive use of force by federal agents.
- 1993 – McVeigh visits Waco, Texas, where police have surrounded a compound which is home to the Branch Davidian cult led by David Koresh. Police troops storm the compound near Waco. The 51-day siege ends but 82 people are killed in the process.
- 1995 – At 09:02 am on 19 April, a van packed with home-made explosives, parked outside the Alfred P Murrah federal building in downtown Oklahoma City explodes. McVeigh is identified and charged with the bombing.
- 1997 – McVeigh is convicted and sentenced to death by lethal injection.
- 2001 – McVeigh is executed by lethal injection at Terre Haute, Indiana, USA.

MORAL BELIEFS

When terrorism is inspired by morality it is driven by a belief that there are rights and wrongs in society. Terrorists of this kind believe that those in power are not taking enough action to punish what they perceive to be as 'wrongdoers'.

Anti-abortion

One such issue of morality is abortion. The US has a long history of anti-abortion activism. In the 1970s and early 1980s, the action largely revolved around non-violent protests. However, in the late 1980s, America began to see the effects of more violent terrorist behaviour such as bombings, burnings, acid attacks and other domestic terrorism. The targets were abortion clinics and the staff working in them.

A wanted man

Eric Robert Rudolph is one of the most notorious anti-abortion terrorists in the US. In 1998 he became one of the FBI's ten most wanted fugitives. He was suspected of carrying out many bombing attempts throughout Atlanta, Georgia, and in particular the Centennial Olympic Park bombing at the 1996 Atlanta Olympics, which killed one and wounded 111 others. Rudolph was finally arrested in May 2003 and was sentenced in July 2005 to five consecutive life sentences.

Animal protection

Another form of moral protest is the case of animal rights. Many animal rights groups campaign against research centres and the agriculture industry. But their cause has often turned to terrorist activities. Groups have been known to vandalise laboratories, steal animals, or use more violent methods such as arson, bombing campaigns and personal threats to employees. The threat of animal activists, such as the Animal Liberation Front, has disrupted the work of many institutions, affecting the safety and morale of workers and costing employers in terms of damage to equipment and the need for increased security measures.

Abortion was legalised in the US in the 1970s. Since that time, many anti-abortion activists have carried out terrorist campaigns to fight for their cause.

AL-QAEDA – Where religious and territorial terrorism collides

Al-Qaeda is the world's first international terrorist network. It offers support for a number of radical Islamic terrorist groups around the world, such as the Harakat ul-Mujahideen in Pakistan and the Islamic Jihad in Egypt. These groups hold deep-rooted resentments about the ownership of land in Muslim countries and about the role of the US and its western allies in the Middle East.

The brainchild of Saudi-born dissident, Osama bin Laden, the al-Qaeda network has organised training camps for thousands of terrorists. Between 15,000 and 20,000 people are believed to have trained at camps in Afghanistan since 1996. The network actively supported the Taliban against the US in Afghanistan in 2001 and is now thought to be involved in the bloody resistance to the US control and restructuring of Iraq.

The destruction of the twin towers of the World Trade Center saw these fanatical terrorists take their terrible acts to the US mainland, and today al-Qaeda has raised the stakes in world terrorism, forcing anti-terrorist security measures that have never been seen before. Although not all recent attacks have been carried out directly by the al-Qaeda network, many terrorist groups are now working hand-in-hand with al-Qaeda, helping to spread its activities throughout the world.

February 1993 – A bomb explodes at the World Trade Center in New York killing six people and injuring more than a thousand. The attack was carried out by an organisation called the Islamic Group, believed to have links with al-Qaeda.

August 1998 – Two truck bombs destroy US embassies in Kenya and Tanzania, leaving 230 dead. Four men linked to al-Qaeda were jailed for life for the attacks.

September 2001 – Nineteen suicide attackers hijack and crash four commercial US jets – two into the World Trade Center, New York, one into the Pentagon, Washington DC, and a fourth into a field in Shanksville, Pennsylvania. The attacks, which claimed more than 3,000 lives, were linked to al-Qaeda.

October 2001 – The US begins a military campaign against al-Qaeda and the Taliban in Afghanistan, in an attempt to stop Afghanistan from remaining a terrorist haven and to find Osama bin Laden. Within three months, the Taliban were effectively ousted and coalition forces have continued to hunt down al-Qaeda militants. To date, Osama bin Laden has not been found.

October 2002 – Two car bomb attacks in Bali kill more than 200 and injure more than 300 others. An Islamic group, Jemaah Islamiah, was blamed for the atrocities. The group is believed to have links with al-Qaeda.

July 2005 – Suicide bombers kill 53 people in four attacks – one bus and three underground trains – in London.

August 2006 – Massive security alert at UK airports countered suspected attacks on flights to USA.

Osama bin Laden and his al-Qaeda network masterminded the September 11th terrorist attacks.

THE TERRORISTS' TOOLS

Terrorists use a multitude of methods to carry out their terror and to achieve their aims. Terrorist atrocities vary from attacks on individuals (such as assassinations or kidnappings) to bomb attacks on large groups of people (such as shoppers in a market or travellers on an aeroplane). Attacks on aeroplanes and other forms of transport have become increasingly popular because they help terrorists to achieve a number of their aims: they disrupt everyday life; they can be very expensive for the economy of the countries being attacked; and they always gain an enormous amount of publicity.

The wreckage of the Lockerbie bomb (left). An investigation found that the devastation was caused by a cassette recorder laden with plastic explosives and activated by a timing device.

Hijacking

The trend for hijacking accelerated in the 1970s when over 30 per cent of terrorist attacks were targeted at aircraft. Soon after, many governments called for stricter controls at airports.

Nevertheless, during the 1990s there were no less than 182 hijackings worldwide and in 2001, the hijacking of four aircraft in the US on September 11th highlighted that hijacking is still a very potent tool for terrorists.

Aeroplanes are also a popular target for bombers.

Explosives, activated by timing devices, can claim the lives of all those onboard. Suicide bombers are also a serious threat. In December 2001, an American Airlines flight made an emergency landing in Boston after a passenger tried to detonate explosives hidden in his shoes. The so-called 'shoe bomber', Richard Reid, was overpowered by passengers and crew. Reid had links with terror suspects, including al-Qaeda and was sentenced to life in prison in 2003. In August 2006, plans to target at least 11 flights from the UK to the US were discovered.

Bombs

Bombs are very popular with terrorists because they are easy to use, easy to transport and have devastating effects. Plastic explosives such as semtex are small, light and odourless. It took just under 1kg of semtex, built into a cassette recorder, to bring down the Pan Am flight over Lockerbie in 1988.

Bombs can also be fitted with timing devices and detonators so that they can be placed in the target area long before they explode. This is what happened in Brighton in 1984, when the Irish Republican Army (IRA) targeted the Brighton Grand Hotel where the Conservative government were staying for their annual party conference. The terrorists planted a 10kg bomb many weeks before the start of the conference to avoid any security checks. The bomb caused massive devastation, killing four people and injuring more than 30. Seven years later, the IRA attacked the British government again when they conducted a mortar attack against 10 Downing Street, injuring two civil servants and two policemen.

Car bombs are also a very common tool for many terrorist groups across the world. This method has been used to assassinate political figures (see page 19) or to cause mass destruction. On 12 October 2002, a car bomb exploded in a busy tourist area in Bali, Indonesia. The attack killed over 200 people from 24 countries. Indonesia is made up of more than 13,000 islands and a number of rebel groups are threatening the country's stability. The Bali bombing was linked to Jemaah Islamiah, an Islamic group with links to al-Qaeda. In 2005, terrorist bombs killed 88 tourists in Egypt. Al-Qaeda is again suspected.

Car bombs have been used to assassinate particular people or to cause mass devastation.

Suicide bombers

One of the most shattering ways that explosives have been used is through the act of a suicide bomber. Suicide bombers detonate explosives which they carry on their body, or drive a vehicle packed with a bomb, killing themselves and people around them. Groups choose to use suicide terrorism because of the fear that it generates and the ability to conduct accurate, large-scale attacks without sophisticated technology.

The Middle East is now dominated by the horror of suicide bombings – since 1994 there have been well over 100 Palestinian suicide bombings in Israel, sparking revenge attacks from Israelis. The bombers have blown up buses, shopping malls, cafes and other civilian targets.

In most cases suicide bombers are motivated by religious fervour. According to Islamic tradition, those who give their life for an Islamic cause will have their sins forgiven and a place reserved in paradise. The family of a suicide bomber often consider their relative to be heroic. Recruits are picked out from mosques, schools and religious institutions. They are likely to have shown particular dedication to the principles of Islam and are singled out for deeper study. Eventually, many of the recruits will volunteer for a suicide mission, hoping for greater glory.

Assassinations

Some terrorist attacks have very specific targets – a group might seek to assassinate an individual who holds radically different views, for example.

In 1979, Shadow Northern Ireland Secretary, Airey Neave, was killed by a car bomb as he left the House of Commons. The Provisional IRA and the INLA (see page 46) targeted the British Conservative MP because of his tough line on anti-IRA security. Neave was killed days before the Conservatives came to power, when he would have joined the British Cabinet.

In October 2001, Palestinian gunmen assassinated far-right Israeli cabinet minster Rehavam Zeevi. Zeevi's extreme political views included advocating the transfer of Palestinians to neighbouring Arab countries. The PFLP (see page 46) took responsibility for the killing – a revenge attack for the assassination by Israel of their leader, Mustafa Ali Zibri.

Hostage takers

Terrorists have also used sieges to try to persuade governments to take actions – such as releasing prisoners or withdrawing from disputed land.

In 1979, a group of radical Iranian students stormed the American Embassy in Tehran, taking staff hostage for over a year. The students were angered by US support for their exiled leader, the Shah. They were forced to give way when the Shah died, but the Iranian government actively backed the siege.

During the 1980s, a number of extremist groups tried to defeat western values in the Middle East. In 1986, Brian Keenan, a teacher at the American University in Beirut, and ten other westerners were captured by Islamic Jihad and other militant groups. Talks between Lebanon, Iran and the West eventually led to their release. Some hostages were held for over five years.

19

Staff at the American Embassy in Tehran were taken hostage by students in 1979. The Iranian government backed the siege.

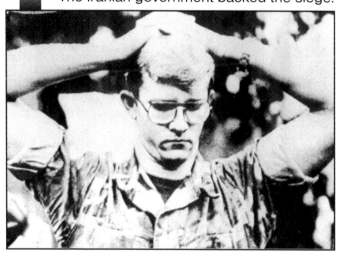

Information

Terrorist groups, such as al-Qaeda, have a long tradition of sharing information and techniques. They might offer training to each other, co-operate with money laundering or facilitate the sale of weapons or essential items such as fake passports. Sometimes, collaboration between terrorists is planned. At other times, the existence of modern communication methods, such as television broadcasting and the internet, means that ideas can be shared very easily.

Al-Qaeda have used training camps in Afghanistan to train future terrorists.

Newspaper reports spread the work of terrorists around the world.

Publicity

The publicity that a terrorist atrocity receives gives added weight to the work of a terrorist. Technological developments mean that reports and graphic images of terrorist attacks can now reach people around the world extremely quickly. When the knowledge spreads, so does fear.

Many people now live in fear of a terrorist threat when the risk to themselves is actually very small. Terrorists have achieved many of their aims if they cause a gridlock of fear amongst ordinary citizens.

Baader-Meinhof

The Baader-Meinhof gang was a terrorist group of young German people who wanted to change the political system of their country. These well educated, middle-class activists were officially known as the Red Army Faction in Germany in the 1970s, when they carried out a series of kidnappings and sieges, robbed banks and bombed buildings.

Tools of the trade

The Baader-Meinhof were initially trained in one of the many Palestinian guerilla camps in the Middle East, which recruited left-wingers from around the world. At the time, the Palestinians were trying to impress internationals so that they would return home and tell everyone about their cause. There were also several Palestinian terror groups active at the time, mostly under the general umbrella of the Palestine Liberation Organisation (PLO). The Baader-Meinhof gang continued to be active until the early 1990s, when the group finally disbanded.

20

THE PROFILE OF A TERRORIST

It is difficult to identify a typical terrorist. People who turn to political violence do so for many different reasons. They may be driven by poverty, a lack of opportunities, oppression or political or religious beliefs. Amongst Palestinians for example, Hamas talent spotters scout for new recruits among the Muslim worshippers in the mosques and among the disillusioned in other Islamic organisations.

Terrorists from wealthy backgrounds

The German Baader-Meinhof gang was one example of a group of middle-class terrorists.

Andreas Baader (1943-77) was the son of a historian. He was drawn towards the left wing student movement and was jailed in 1968 for his involvement in a bomb attack in Frankfurt. Baader escaped from police custody in 1970 with the help of Ulrike Meinhof. Together they formed the Red Army Faction but were captured in 1972 during a siege of the West German embassy in Stockholm. Baader committed suicide in 1977 after starting a life sentence.

Ulrike Meinhof (1934-76) was the daughter of an art historian. She graduated in philosophy and sociology and was a writer for left wing magazines. Meinhof formed the Red Army Faction with Andreas Baader but was captured by police in 1972. She committed suicide in 1976 whilst on trial.

Osama bin Laden, leader of the al-Qaeda network.

Different backgrounds

Terrorists have also come from wealthy, well educated and privileged backgrounds. For example, Osama bin Laden, the mastermind behind the al-Qaeda network (see page 16), is the son of the Yemeni-born owner of a leading Saudi construction company. He was born into great wealth and it is believed that he inherited as much as $300 million when his father died in the 1960s. As leader of the world's first international terrorist network, Osama bin Laden is the world's most wanted terrorist with a bounty of $25 million on his head.

Terrorist groups in Israel recruit young people who show a particular dedication to Islam. They are trained and may later sacrifice themselves as suicide bombers.

A lawyer's son

Mohammed Atta, one of the key terrorists who hijacked one of the planes that crashed into the World Trade Center on 11 September 2001, was from a wealthy background – he was the son of a successful lawyer and grew up in a middle-class Cairo neighbourhood. He does not fit the mould of the young Muslim suicide bombers raised in Lebanon and the Palestinian territories.

A young girl

Shinaz Amuri was the first female suicide bomber in Israel, and probably the first in contemporary terrorism. On 27 January 2002, she triggered an explosion that ripped through Jerusalem, killing herself, an 81-year-old man and injuring more than 100 others. Amuri was in her twenties and a student at Al-Najah University in the West Bank town of Nablus, a Hamas stronghold.

What is a terrorist wing?

The political nature of terrorism means that political groups and terrorist groups are often closely linked. The term 'terrorist wing' describes a terrorist group that is associated with a non-violent political group. While political groups use the political system to bring about change, terrorist wings resort to force and violence.

Hamas is the Palestinians' major fundamentalist movement, and is now the ruling party. It has a political wing which is concerned with the education of Muslim children and other social projects. But Hamas also has a well-known terrorist wing that plots suicide bombings in Israel.

In Northern Ireland, the political party Sinn Fein opposed British rule in Northern Ireland. Sinn Fein's terrorist wing, the IRA, killed around 1,800 people, between the late 1960s and early 1990s. Although the IRA declared a cease-fire in 1994, some splinter groups are still active. Today, real progress has been made. The terrorist wing has laid down arms and Sinn Fein has joined the government.

WOMEN AND TERRORISM

Women have always participated in terrorism. But traditionally they have rarely been involved in internal discipline or punishment within their organisations, or acts of violence, such as carrying out suicide bombings. However, times are changing. Until 2002, when female suicide bomber, Shinaz Amuri, brought devastation in Jerusalem, the only active female suicide bombers were those of the Tamil Tiger terrorists in Sri Lanka. Today, the innocent appearance of women is being used as a tactic by more and more terrorist groups.

Female recruits are now common in organisations such as the Basque Fatherland and Liberty (ETA) in Spain and the Revolutionary Armed Forces of Colombia (FARC) (see page 46). An influx of women has enabled terrorist groups to disguise themselves better, since a woman on her own, or a couple, are less likely to raise suspicion than two men operating together.

Keeping the peace

Women have also played a key role in attempts to resolve the problems of terrorism. In the US, women are now being used as interrogators of al-Qaeda suspects. In Northern Ireland, women have also been used to facilitate the ongoing peace process. In 1996, Monica McWilliams and Pearl Sagar, from the Northern Ireland Women's Coalition were elected to multi-party talks on the future of Northern Ireland. At the negotiating table, McWilliams and Sager sought to bring a new approach to the troubles. They championed for integrated education and housing, the creation of a Civic Forum and support for victims of violence.

Leila Khaled

Palestinian-born Leila Khaled became a household name in 1970 when she was held in the UK during the international hijacking crisis, known now as Black September.

Khaled had led an attempted hijacking of an Israeli El Al flight from Amsterdam but was overpowered and arrested on arrival in the UK. She was released in exchange for western hostages held by the Popular Front for the Liberation of Palestine (PFLP).

Born into a large family in Haifa, Khaled was only four years old when she was forced along with her mother, seven sisters and five brothers to leave Palestine when it was partitioned in 1948. From a young age she committed herself to armed struggle for the Palestinian cause.

Women in Black is a worldwide network of women who are committed to peace with justice and actively opposed to war and other forms of violence. Their actions are generally women only, and often take the form of women wearing black, standing in public places to conduct silent, non-violent vigils at regular times and intervals, carrying placards and handing out leaflets.

Woman in Black vigils started in Israel in 1988 by women protesting against Israel's occupation of the West Bank and the Gaza Strip, demanding peace between Israelis and Palestinians. Italian supporters of the Israeli women took the idea back to Italy – and so the idea has spread around the world.

Women in Black groups demonstrate to give a sense of solidarity and purpose to women, to lend support to women around the world who are close to violence, and to educate, inform and influence public opinion to try to make war an unthinkable option.

Women in Israel (above) and Iraq (top) have been using forms of non-violent demonstration to draw attention to the terrorist atrocities in their country. They live in hope of a peaceful world for all (right).

GLOBAL MAP OF TERRORISM

There is no continent on earth that is entirely free from terrorism. Countries in the developed world, such as America and parts of Europe, are vulnerable to terrorism because of their emphasis on personal freedoms and their easy targets such as transport and supplies of water, electricity or fuel. The free and widespread media in these countries also maximises the potential for terrorist publicity, and terrorist messages are likely to reach a large number of people.

The developing world

There is extensive media coverage of terrorist activity in the developed world, but the world's less developed nations are actually experiencing higher rates of terrorist attacks. Many developing countries have weak central governments and are susceptible to bouts of civil war. These are ideal conditions for powerful guerrillas and paramilitary groups, most of whom oppose the ruling elite, to seek power through force and the use of terror. According to US government figures, Colombia suffered the most terrorist attacks in 2002, followed closely by India and Angola.

A growing problem

Domestic terrorism is a continuing problem in many of the war-torn parts of the globe, but today, the alarming increase in international terrorism is a major concern for world leaders. Terrorist groups around the world, like al-Qaeda, have grown to support each other in their training and in their methods. Many groups are also finding a common cause to which they can unite, such as Islamic Fundamentalism. Terrorism is no longer confined to traditional 'trouble spots'.

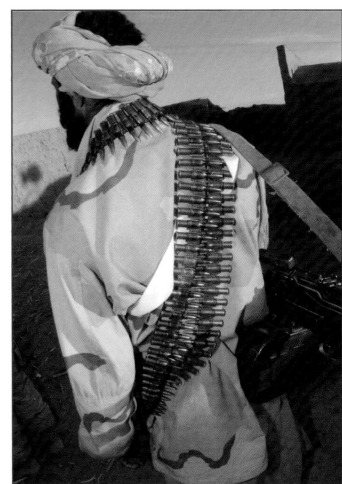

The fight against the Taliban in 2001 saw the United States and Great Britain unite with the Northern Alliance, in their search for al-Qaeda suspects. In 2006, an international peace-keeping force suffered casualties fighting against the Taliban. Around the world, countries are now uniting in their efforts to combat terrorism.

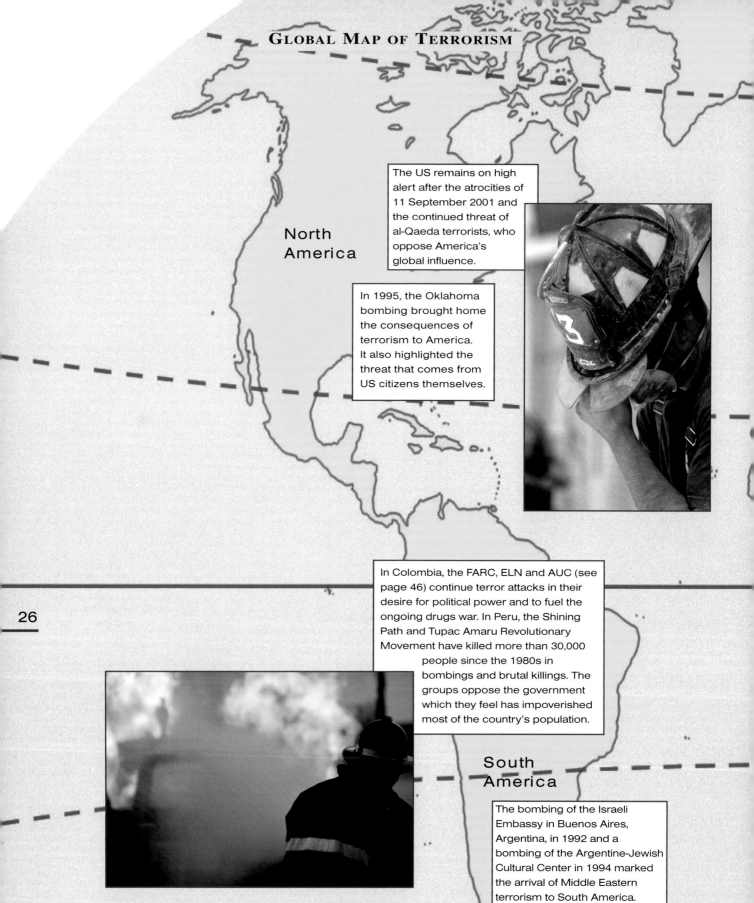

North
America

The US remains on high
alert after the atrocities of
11 September 2001 and
the continued threat of
al-Qaeda terrorists, who
oppose America's
global influence.

In 1995, the Oklahoma
bombing brought home
the consequences of
terrorism to America.
It also highlighted the
threat that comes from
US citizens themselves.

In Colombia, the FARC, ELN and AUC (see
page 46) continue terror attacks in their
desire for political power and to fuel the
ongoing drugs war. In Peru, the Shining
Path and Tupac Amaru Revolutionary
Movement have killed more than 30,000
people since the 1980s in
bombings and brutal killings. The
groups oppose the government
which they feel has impoverished
most of the country's population.

South
America

The bombing of the Israeli
Embassy in Buenos Aires,
Argentina, in 1992 and a
bombing of the Argentine-Jewish
Cultural Center in 1994 marked
the arrival of Middle Eastern
terrorism to South America.

GLOBAL MAP OF TERRORISM

On 7 July 2005, London commuters became the target for suicide bombers. Linked to al-Qaeda, they bombed three underground trains and a bus, killing 53 people.

Russia

Europe

Chechen rebels have carried out a series of suicide bombings and kidnaps against Russia in their desire for independence.

In 1995, the Aum Shinrikyo doomsday cult carried out a sarin gas attack on the subway system in Tokyo, Japan, killing 12 people and injuring more than 5,000.

The ETA have carried out a series of bloody attacks in Spain and France since the 1950s. The group wants to create a Basque homeland in Spain.

Osama bin Laden's al-Qaeda network continue to be active in the Middle East, including Iraq. The Middle East peace process is in tatters after all-out conflict between Israel and Hezbollah in Lebanon.

Pakistani-backed terrorists are thought to be responsible for the 2006 bombings of trains in Mumbai, India, killing 182 people.

Asia

Africa

Terrorists in Egypt killed more than 88 people at a holiday resort in 2005. It is thought that al-Qaeda was behind the attacks. Many African countries are also subject to civil unrest and domestic terrorism.

The Tamil Tigers have carried out more than 200 suicide bombings since the late 1980s. The group seeks an independent state in areas of Sri Lanka inhabited by a minority group of ethnic Tamils.

Jemaah Islamiah has been blamed for the 2002 Bali bombing in Indonesia. The group, which has links with al-Qaeda, seeks an Islamic state incorporating Indonesia, Malaysia, and the southern Philippines.

27

Australia

Terrorism around the world

From east to west, and north to south, terrorism is a very real threat to countries of the modern world. Domestic terrorism has now been joined by terrorism that is largely motivated by international networks.

THE FIGHT AGAINST TERRORISTS

There is no certain way to combat terrorism. Short-term measures include the tightening of security after specific terrorist warnings and the use of 'alert' warnings in a particular country. Until a long-term solution is found, intelligence gathering is vital in the fight against terrorism.

Intelligence helps governments to assess the activities of terrorist groups around the world.

Anti-terrorist police

The increase in global terrorism in recent years has led to a shift in policing priorities around the world. Additional resources have been given to dedicated anti-terrorist police who are trained to be prepared for terrorist atrocities, to gather intelligence about terrorist activities and to foil attempted terrorist attacks.

Secret intelligence

One of the most effective ways of limiting terrorist activities is through secret information or 'intelligence'. Intelligence is gathered from 'open' sources (such as newspapers and media broadcasts), diplomatic relations and secret sources (such as espionage or other informers). Intelligence agencies also gather information from satellites and aeroplane photography and by using telephone or email tracking devices. Terrorists rely on money to carry out their activities, so freezing the financial assets of suspect terrorist backers is another method that governments use to disable the work of terrorist groups. Intelligence is being gathered every day to alert governments to forthcoming terrorist activities.

Reducing the risk

In the event of a terrorist attack, anti-terrorist police and other government agencies have established emergency measures to reduce the impact of an atrocity. In the UK, after a series of anthrax attacks in the US, there was a very public stockpiling of anthrax vaccine. Emergency teams also carry out regular drills to practise strategies in the event that a major evacuation is needed. Meanwhile, measures are taken to tighten border controls and to increase security on public transport – at airports and stations – and in other public areas. In Britain, public spaces are monitored with an estimated 1.5 million closed-circuit cameras.

Anti-terrorist police carry out regular training to improve their anti-terrorist strategies.

Reacting to a threat

After September 11th, many countries developed in-depth security and emergency measures to counteract the terrorist threat. In the 2005 attacks on the London public transport system, many shortcomings were highlighted. It has prompted a review of security at the stations, the underground communications equipment and the response time of emergency services. New plans are being implemented at underground stations to try to prevent a repeat of these events.

In August 2006, the threat of multiple airliner bombings prompted a radical review of all passenger carry-on luggage.

Preventing atrocities

The work of anti-terrorist police has led to a number of foiled terrorist attacks. In January 2003, an intelligence tip-off led to the arrest of six Algerian men at a flat in north London. Anti-terrorist police found small quantities of the potentially lethal poison, ricin, at the property and the men were held for questioning.

In June 2003, Kenyan police foiled an al-Qaeda plot intending to destroy the US Embassy in Nairobi with a truck bomb and a hijacked plane loaded with explosives. The tip-off arose during the interrogation of terror suspect, Salmin Mohammed Khamis. Once a terrorist alert was issued, Kenyan officials banned flights to Somalia and the US Embassy was closed for four days. Khamis and three other suspects were later tried for conspiring to commit a number of terrorist attacks in Kenya since 1998.

In Israel, sniffer dogs are trained to detect suicide bombers and explosives on public transport.

Long-term measures

Politicians are also looking at long-term strategies to help reduce the threat of terrorism. In countries where territory is being disputed, such as Israel, nations have tried to introduce a peace process to bring the countries involved to the negotiating table.

In Israel, the peace process has periodically gained momentum, only to be set back by a resurgence of terrorist activity months later. However, in other parts of the world, such as South Africa and Northern Ireland, peace talks have helped to reduce levels of terrorism (see pages 34-38). These models have encouraged other nations to take the road to peace.

Terrorism and the law

Political violence usually comes about when all other avenues are closed. When people suffer oppression or are denied a peaceful and legal route to justice and social change, they may turn to force if they have exhausted all other tactics.

This was the route that the African National Congress (ANC) took in the the early 1960s (see page 37) when peaceful protests had come to nothing. As long as groups continue to feel oppressed or ignored, the world is guaranteed to see new terrorists, freedom fighters, or justice groups emerge.

In the long-term, the 'war' on terrorism will only be won when all people have the ability to consider the point of view of others, and to share the same values of human life regardless of political, religious or moral beliefs. A key part of that process is the development of a genuinely global economic and political democracy.

Such a system would allow all people to openly speak about economic, political, religious and moral beliefs, without fear or oppression.

 ## How do you think the public could help?

• Anti-terrorist police request that the public co-operate on mattters of national security.
• They ask that the public remain vigilant for suspect bags, packages, vehicles, or people acting suspiciously at stations and airports.
• The public should report anything suspicious to the police or the appropriate authorities.
• The police also ask that the public co-operate in the event of an attack – following the instructions of those in charge of the emergency.

TERRORISM AND HUMAN RIGHTS

The rise in terrorism across the globe, and the effects of September 11th in particular, has led to extreme measures to try to control the threat of terrorists. While governments around the world have introduced forceful anti-terrorism laws, human rights campaigners have argued that individual freedoms have been sacrificed in many highly publicised attempts to crack down on terrorism.

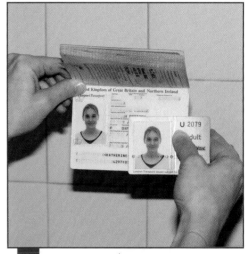

In many countries, citizens are required to carry national identity cards.

Just weeks after the September 11th attacks, the US Congress overwhelmingly passed a new piece of legislation called the USA Patriot Act. Many argue that the Act places severe restrictions on freedom of speech by creating a definition of 'domestic terrorism' that includes acts that 'appear to be intended to influence the policy of a government by intimidation or coercion'. Such acts could include peaceful mass demonstrations and other non-violent protest. The Act also gives wide ranging powers to the state – such as tracking emails and use of the internet, and obtaining education and medical records, without the need for an individual's consent.

Guantanamo Bay

Following the 2001 conflict in Afghanistan, the US have been holding over 600 people from more than 40 different nationalities, at a US naval base in Guantanamo Bay, Cuba. Many of the detainees are Taliban fighters or al-Qaeda suspects. Because the detainees are not legally prisoners of war, the US are not bound by the Geneva Convention. However, human rights groups have called for the prisoners' release, and in 2006 the USA announced that it would close Guantanamo Bay.

Detainees at Camp X-Ray, the US naval base in Guantanamo Bay, Cuba, are being held by the US without access to any court, legal counsel or family visits.

In 2004, China began to issue a series of electronic identity cards for its 960 million citizens.

Additional terrorist legislation

Other countries have passed legislation in an attempt to tighten up security in their homeland. In India, the 2002 Prevention of Terrorism Act allows police to hold suspects without charge. It also criminalises the act of journalists meeting with any member of a 'terrorist organization', whatever the purpose.

In China, Beijing has intensified its campaign against Islamic separatists in Xinjiang province – which borders on Afghanistan, Pakistan and Central Asia – claiming that these Muslims are linked to 'international terrorism'. There are now reports that new restrictions have been placed on the religious rights of Muslims in China.

In 2002, Australia passed a series of anti-terrorism laws. The legislation included strengthening the powers of the Australian Security Intelligence Organisation (ASIO) and criminalising membership of a terrorist organisation.

Tightening security measures

In Turkey, atrocities by Kurdish separatists and Islamic militants have been used to justify tapping into telephone conversations and raiding private homes, causing outrage by human rights groups.

In many European countries, such as Germany, Belgium and Spain, citizens are required to carry national identity (ID) cards. The cards were originally designed to control immigration and the use of social services, but in the wake of terrorist atrocities, their scope has been increased to provide an additional level of national security. Human rights groups are against such forms of identification, claiming that in a free society citizens are entitled to a certain level of privacy.

When is a killer a terrorist or a murderer?

There are many organised groups and movements around the world that have embarked upon mass killings and the terrorising of innocent people.

The Italian Mafia is one of the world's most established criminal organisations, and one of the most serious social problems

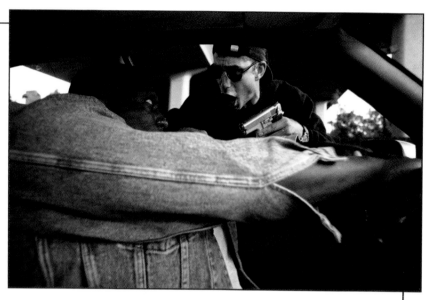

confronting Italy today. The Mafia place themselves above the law and Mafia groups have murdered judges, priests and children in a series of personal vendettas. Some argue that Mafia groups, unlike terrorists, are not designed to change the existing political order, but are involved in purely criminal activities, such as murder.

Curtailment of freedom

Across the world, new restrictions on movement and the freedom of speech have generally been accepted because of the fear of terrorism. However, this is not a new development. During the height of the IRA activity in mainland Britain in the 1970s and 80s, many civil rights were disregarded. Britain detained terrorist suspects for up to seven days without charge and denied them a trial by jury.

In March 1988, the British SAS shot dead three unarmed IRA members in Gibraltar. A car was reported to be packed with explosives near the British Governor's residence and the British soldiers acted because they thought they were in danger. Britain was forced to admit that the three IRA members were unarmed and in September 1995, the European Court of Human Rights concluded that Britain had breached the European Convention on Human Rights.

Human Rights and the United Nations (UN)

• In 1945, the UN's founding nations resolved that the horrors of the Second World War should never be allowed to recur.
• In 1948, they passed the 'Universal Declaration of Human Rights' which states that respect for human rights and human dignity 'is the foundation of freedom, justice and peace in the world'.
• The UN has since developed International Human Rights standards to protect people's rights against violations by individuals, groups or nations. These conventions include measures against genocide, torture and discrimination against race, women or children.
• Each year the UN works with governments from approximately 100 nations. The UN monitors the situation in each country and offers recommendations for improvements in the area of human rights.
• Dialogue between different nations and the UN has led to many concrete results, such as the suspension of executions, release of detainees and medical treatment for prisoners, as well as changes of domestic legal systems.

33

SOLUTIONS AND SUCCESSES

Peace talks have successfully ended a number of long-term terrorist campaigns. Confronted by the threat of continuing terrorism, elected politicians have to decide whether some of the grievances that drive ordinary people to join terrorist organisations are in any way justifiable and legitimate. They may have to accept causes for previous acts of terrorism without giving in to all uses of the violence, in order to encourage parties to start peace discussions.

Some governments have used peace talks to overcome the problems of terrorism.

NORTHERN IRELAND

In the early 1990s, peace talks began in an attempt to resolve the ongoing conflict between Catholics and Protestants in Northern Ireland. In December 1995, former US senator George Mitchell was appointed to serve as a mediator and the talks resulted in the Good Friday Agreement in 1998.

The Agreement was a call for peace by the British and Irish governments and most of the main political parties in Northern Ireland, including Sinn Fein, the political arm of the Irish Republican Army (IRA),

took part. Sinn Fein had long been associated with terrorism but an IRA cease-fire in 1994 brought the political group to the negotiating table.

The Good Friday Agreement advocated that minority Catholics in Northern Ireland should have a share of the political power, and the Republic of Ireland should have a voice in Northern Irish affairs. In return, Catholics were to give up their goal of a united Ireland unless the largely Protestant North voted in favour of it.

The negotations saw Britain accepting that they could not defeat terrorism in Northern Ireland militarily. Despite being linked with terrorism for many years, Sinn Fein also came to the conclusion that they had more to gain by moving away from terrorism.

Although linked to terrorism, Sinn Fein leader, Gerry Adams (centre), actively sought to involve his party in the Northern Ireland peace talks.

The Irish Story

Ireland has had a turbulent relationship with mainland Britain for nearly 800 years. Henry II of England invaded the country in the 12th century. Ireland was later colonised and a series of independence movements through the ages were met with violent opposition.

There have always been defiant organisations wishing to return Ireland to complete self-rule. In 1916, Irish Nationalists seized the General Post Office in Dublin and declared an independent Irish Republic. The so-called 'Easter Rising' was crushed by the British who executed its leaders. Irish public opinion was outraged and a long and bitter battle began.

Catholic and Protestant groups have been actively involved in terrorism in Northern Ireland. More than 3,600 people on both sides have died since what the Irish call 'the troubles' began in 1969.

Living side by side in Northern Ireland

• There are two main groups of people in Northern Ireland – Unionists (mainly Protestants who have traditionally wanted Northern Ireland to stay part of the UK) and Republicans (mainly Catholics who have wanted Northern Ireland to rejoin the Republic of Ireland).

• There are terrorist groups associated with both Unionists (eg the UDA, UVF and UFF) and Republicans (eg the IRA and the INLA) (see page 46).

• The IRA agreed to a cease-fire in 1994, but splinter groups still remained active. The so-called 'Real IRA' was responsible for the Omagh bomb of 1998. Unionist groups also continued with violence – in 1998 the LVF killed the nephew of Sinn Fein leader, Gerry Adams.

• In October 2001, the IRA began to disarm – an action that Unionists had long demanded as proof of the IRA's commitment to peace. However, two IRA splinter groups, the Real IRA and the Continuity IRA, were still practising terrorism in 2003.

• In 2006, broad agreement was reached to reopen the Northern Ireland Assembly.

The following years were littered with political negotiations, combined with terrorist activity from the Irish Republican Army.

In 1920, following negotiations, the British and some Irish agreed to split Ireland into two. An independent state was created in the island's predominantly Catholic south and a smaller, northern district, with a Protestant majority, remained part of the United Kingdom.

The formation of Northern Ireland caused widespread violence and terrorism for most of the 20th century. Many Catholics have complained of feeling like second-class citizens in Northern Ireland and have backed the Republicans in their quest for a united Ireland, free from British rule. On the other side, Protestants want to stay loyal to Britain and have opposed the Republican desire to expel the British and form a united Ireland.

The Good Friday Agreement was jeopardized in October 2002 when the British government suspended Northern Ireland's power-sharing government because of allegations that Sinn Fein members were involved in an IRA spy-ring. There were also reports that the IRA had failed to disarm.

Despite the grid-lock in the peace process, new negotiations began in 2004 for a review of the Good Friday Agreement. Many political parties, including Sinn Fein, want the Agreement to stay, but Northern Ireland's largest party, the Democratic Unionist Party (DUP) are demanding that the Agreement is scrapped.

Britain is still optimistic that self-rule can be restored to Northern Ireland, and there appears to be no threat of a resurgence of terrorist violence. In 2003 there were 10 killings attributed to political activity – the third lowest number since 1969, when violence broke out on a wide scale. Meanwhile, the negotiations are continuing and there is real hope that eventually there will be a lasting democratic solution to the troubles.

Good Friday Agreement

• On Good Friday, 10 April 1998, a landmark agreement was made to secure peace in Northern Ireland. The Agreement followed thirty years of conflict in which several thousand Protestants and Catholics had been killed, and more than 30,000 injured.

• The result was the Belfast Agreement, which is commonly known as the Good Friday Agreement.

• The Good Friday Agreement involved constitutional change in the Republic of Ireland which meant the end of Britain's territorial claim to Northern Ireland. It also established a Northern Ireland Assembly based on power-sharing.

• In December 1999, a legislative Assembly of both Unionist and Republican politicians was finally set up to share power in Northern Ireland, with Ministers and committee members drawn from both sides of the political divide.

• In October 2002, the British government suspended Northern Ireland's power-sharing government.

• Peace talks continue and in 2006, progress was made with the intention to reopen the Northern Ireland Assembly at Stormont.

Pallbearers carry a victim of the Omagh bombing in Northern Ireland, 1998. Despite an IRA cease-fire in 1994, the atrocity was linked to a splinter group known as the 'Real IRA'.

A changing South Africa

In 1912, tribal chiefs gathered together with community and church organisations to form the African National Congress (ANC). The ANC wanted to defend the rights and freedoms of black South Africans. The ANC started as a peaceful organisation but as the South African government's policies became more oppressive towards black communities, the ANC turned to more violent methods.

The ANC was formed at a time when South Africa was changing very fast. Diamonds and gold had been discovered in the late 1800s and many blacks were forced to leave their land to work in the mines. During the Second World War, manufacturing in towns and cities also grew to meet the wartime demand. By 1946 many blacks lived in squatter communities on the outskirts of major cities.

SOUTH AFRICA

European settlers arrived in South Africa in the 1600s and the country was later colonised by Britain in the 1800s. Disputes between black South Africans and their white counterparts are very deep-rooted. However, they were aggravated further in the 20th century when South African governments, led by white South Africans, greatly strengthened white control of the country. Successive governments carried out a policy – commonly known as 'apartheid' – which discriminated against black citizens. There were attempts at peaceful protest and persuasion to stop the injustice. However, the situation only grew worse and in the 1940s the African National Congress (ANC) started a 'defiance campaign'.

Peace turning to violence

The government accused the ANC of communism and arrested leading members of the organisation. Peaceful protests continued in the 1950s but peace turned to anger when, in March 1960, a non-violent protest at Sharpville, by a group linked to the ANC, saw police open fire, killing 70 protesters and

The government of South Africa carried out a policy of apartheid for much of the 20th century. Black South Africans were discriminated against in many parts of society.

injuring almost 200. The ANC took up arms against the government because they believed that peaceful protest alone would not force the regime to change.

In the following years the ANC carried out many acts of sabotage. In 1964, ANC leader Nelson Mandela was arrested and convicted of sabotage and plotting to overthrow the government. He was imprisoned for 27 years. The ANC decided to continue violent methods of protest with further bombings and acts of sabotage.

In the 1980s the struggle went to new heights. The ANC were showing more signs of strong resistance and the 'Free Mandela' campaign had begun. In spite of government oppression, the mass movement took to the city streets defiantly. The people proclaimed the ANC were a legitimate force. In February 1990, the South African government was forced to lift their ban on the ANC and other organisations. It was clear the tide was turning. World opinion was now pressing for stronger actions against the racist South African government. People from around the world were also calling for Mandela's release.

Mandela's release

In 1990, Nelson Mandela (left) was freed after 27 years in prison and the South African government began negotiations with the ANC. In 1991, Mandela was elected President of the ANC. The negotiations, initiated by the ANC, resulted in the first multiracial elections in South Africa, based on one person one vote, in April 1994. The ANC won these elections with a vast majority. More than 60 per cent of the 22 million votes cast were in favour of the ANC.

In May 1994 Nelson Mandela was inaugurated as the President of South Africa. The man who started out as a freedom fighter and paid the price of terrorism with 27 years in jail, became the elected leader of the country he had spent his entire life trying to liberate. In a meeting to celebrate Nelson Mandela's 85th birthday in July 2003, the British Prime Minister stated that Mandela 'symbolised the triumph of hope over injustice'.

Can a terrorist be the same as a freedom fighter?

The ANC wanted to bring about equal pay, housing and conditions for black people, but they killed many people in the process. Can their actions be justified?

How you define a group largely depends on whether you think the group's ends justify its violent means. Some saw the ANC as terrorists, others viewed their attacks as a legitimate part of the struggle against apartheid. Because terrorism is a tactic and 'freedom fighting' describes a motivation, it is possible for a person, or group, to be both terrorists and freedom fighters at the same time.

38

THE NEW AGE OF TERRORISM

In the months that followed September 11th and July 7th, increased media attention heightened the public's awareness of new terrorist threats. For some years, terrorists have been developing technology and chemical or biological weapons because they are cheaper to manufacture and can quickly wreak havoc on a massive scale. As the focus on mass terrorism continues, governments in the western world are keen to show their citizens that precautions are being taken.

Today's weapons

Nowadays, nuclear, biological and chemical weapons are becoming more common because the materials are easier to obtain. One of the biggest threats is the 'dirty' bomb which spreads nuclear fall-out over a limited area. Other threats include the release of deadly chemicals or bacteria such as anthrax, ricin or smallpox. While nuclear and biological weapons can cause widespread damage, chemical weapons are often used against more specific targets.

Subway attack

Biological terrorism is nothing new. In 1995, Aum Shinrikyo, a Japanese religious cult, made the headlines when some of its members released sarin, a deadly nerve gas, into the Tokyo subway system, killing 12 people and injuring more than 5,000. It is believed that the cult carried out their attack in an attempt to fulfill their belief that the end of the world was near. Their actions showed the world just how easy it is for a small cult or group of terrorists, with limited means, to engage in chemical warfare.

Emergency teams wear protective clothing, like gas masks, when dealing with the threat of chemical or biological attack.

What is anthrax?

Anthrax is a serious disease caused by the bacteria *Bacillus anthracis.* Anthrax is found naturally in the soil and was commonly a hazard for workers who were exposed to infected animals. Today, anthrax can also be made in research laboratories. Anthrax spores can enter the body through cuts in the skin, breathing into the lungs or eating contaminated food. Anthrax is treated with antibiotics.

Improved global communications have helped governments to track down and counteract terrorists. However, telecommunications and computer networks have also helped terrorists to organise, recruit and plan their activities. Modern technology can even be a potential target for terrorists. In a world that has become increasingly dependent on computer technology, attacks on electronic equipment can cause widespread devastation.

Cyberterrorists sabotage electrical equipment, without crossing borders or by-passing security.

40

Cyberterrorism

Cyberterrorism is a term used to describe any terrorist attack that interferes with computers, networks or the information they contain. Small groups, with minimal funds, can use ordinary computer equipment and widely available software to disrupt daily life. They can interrupt electronic equipment with electromagnetic pulses, or destroy computer files altogether with high-emission radio frequency guns.

Cyberterrorists can operate across borders without having to reveal their identity and location. Targets include power stations, military communications, emergency services, traffic control centres, banks and telecommunication networks. Some individuals may choose to conduct cyberterrorism for their own

reasons. However, it is also likely that large scale terrorist organisations, such as al-Qaeda, could use cyberterrorism to enhance the impact of a conventional attack. For example, a terrorist group might seek to disrupt emergency services in the event of a chemical, biological or nuclear attack, to cause maximum devastation.

What is sarin?

Sarin is a highly toxic and volatile nerve agent developed by Nazi scientists in Germany in the 1930s. Sarin comes in both liquid and gas forms and can be inhaled or absorbed through the skin. Although sarin is very complex and dangerous to make, experts say that the gas can be produced by a trained chemist with chemicals that are available to the public. In high doses, sarin suffocates its victims by paralysing the muscles around their lungs.

Weapons of mass destruction

The term 'weapons of mass destruction' – often used in the media – refers to weapons that are capable of causing widespread devastation and mass casualties. Weapons of mass destruction include nuclear, chemical and biological weapons. A nuclear bomb can destroy an entire city. A 'dirty' bomb, which contains some radioactive element, makes an area too dangerous to live in. Biological and chemical attacks include the release of poisonous toxins or bacteria, such as anthrax, into the environment.

What is a dirty bomb?

The main type of dirty bomb combines a conventional explosive, such as dynamite, with radioactive material. Such a bomb could fit into the size of a suitcase (below). If the bomb explodes, there is a risk of both direct casualties and illness caused by exposure to radioactive material. Radiation destroys cells it comes into contact with and is most dangerous when it is swallowed, inhaled or enters an open wound. Radiation is also linked to cancer.

A second type of dirty bomb might involve a more powerful radioactive material being hidden in a public place where people passing close to the source might be subjected to a dangerous dose of radiation.

Decontamination showers are used to remove chemical or biological agents in the event of an attack.

Al-Qaeda and Iraq   41

The greatest threat of chemical, biological or nuclear terrorism appears to come from the al-Qaeda network. Many believe that the events of September 11th show that modern terrorists are willing to kill on a massive scale. Furthermore, Osama bin Laden has already claimed that his group possesses nuclear and chemical weapons.

The belief that Saddam Hussein was assisting al-Qaeda by manufacturing 'weapons of mass destruction' was one of the reasons given for the war on Iraq by the US and allied forces in 2003. There has so far been no hard evidence of stocks of weapons in Iraq. However, al-Qaeda have claimed to be responsible for some of the recent suicide bombings against US soldiers and Iraqi civilians.

WHAT DOES THE FUTURE HOLD?

Terrorism has been around throughout history and sadly there is no certainty that the problem will go away. It is an unfortunate fact that there will always be disagreements in the world. Just as the causes of terrorism arise over many years, it takes generations to unravel the issues involved and to find some kind of solution. But time is a healer. Many major disputes involving terrorist activities have been resolved in recent years. Who would have thought ten years ago that Northern Ireland would ever see peace on the streets again?

We have seen that many interrelated factors play a role in motivating a terrorist group to action. At any time, and in any country of the world, there will always be disputes about religion, politics, land occupation or morality. Terrorist groups also act within a political, cultural and historical context. The African National Congress turned to violence in South Africa because black South Africans faced discrimination at a time when they could see that other citizens around the world were accustomed to freedom.

Negotiations and solutions

There is no single solution to a set of diverse and complicated causes. To date, conflicts have only been resolved when a number of solutions have addressed the specific problems of a particular time and place. Negotiations in Northern Ireland and South Africa have made progress, but a different combination needs to be found in the case of Israelis and Palestinians, or when tackling the threat of al-Qaeda. Inevitably,

an element of compromise will need to be found on either side. It may take some time, but history has proven that it is possible.

In any part of the world, terrorism can cause dreadful destruction and suffering.

42

Gathering intelligence is vital to prevent terrorist attacks, like the events of 11 September 2001, recurring.

Deterrence

In the meantime, the work of deterring terrorism, of gathering intelligence and of catching terrorists is vital. Governments around the world must work together in order to continually stay one step ahead of terrorist groups.

The September 11th attacks changed the way that the world looks at the problem of terrorism. The fear and awareness of terrorism is now greater than ever. However, it is important to keep things in perspective. The vast majority of people will never, in their entire lifetime, come anywhere near to an act of terrorism. Statistics show that the number of people affected by terrorist attacks are greatly outnumbered by the number involved in road traffic accidents every year. The closest that most of us will ever get to an act of terrorism will still be the television pictures that make these acts of violence feel like a real part of our lives.

If history is repeated, future generations may see a resolution to many of today's terrorist conflicts.

CHRONOLOGY

November 1605 – English Catholics attempted to blow up the English Parliament in protest against their King, James I, who was persecuting Catholics.

1795-1799 – The French Revolution, a period that saw the execution of many presumed enemies of the French government. The Revolution coined the term 'terrorism'.

November 1920 – British soldiers opened fire on a crowd at a football match in Dublin, killing 12. The soldiers (or 'Black and Tans') were sent by the British government to control the 'rebel' population there.

December 1920 – The British Parliament and some Irish agreed to split Ireland into one predominantly Catholic region in the south and one predominantly Protestant region in the north. The split caused widespread violence for most of the 20th century.

May 1948 – The United Nations (UN) divided Palestine into two states – Palestine and Israel. The split added to a bitter resentment between Israelis and Palestinians and has resulted in many acts of terrorism.

September 1963 – The United Nations (UN) began work on the elimination of terrorism with the drawing up of the 'Convention on Offenses and Certain Acts Committed On Board Aircraft'. Twelve further conventions relating to terrorism have now been drawn up by the UN.

June 1964 – Nelson Mandela, leader of the African National Congress (ANC), was jailed for life for acts of sabotage and plotting to overthrow the South African government. Mandela was released 27 years later.

March 1979 – British politician, Airey Neave, was killed by a car bomb as he left the House of Commons. IRA-splinter groups were held responsible.

October 1984 – An IRA bomb caused devastation to the Grand Hotel in Brighton, UK, during the Conservative government's annual party conference. Four people were killed and over 30 injured.

April 1986 – Brian Keenan was the first of over ten westerners captured by Islamic Jihad and other militant groups in Lebanon. Some of the hostages were held for over five years.

December 1988 – Libyan terrorists smuggled a bomb onto Pan Am Flight 103 which exploded over Lockerbie, Scotland, UK. All 259 people on board were killed, as well as 11 people on the ground.

February 1991 – An IRA-led mortar attack on 10 Downing Street narrowly missed MPs meeting in the Cabinet room. Four staff were injured.

April 1992 – A bombing of the Israeli Embassy in Buenos Aires, Argentina, marked the arrival of Middle Eastern terrorism to South America.

February 1993 – A car bomb, planted by Islamic terrorists, exploded in an underground car park at the World Trade Center, New York City, killing six and injuring more than 1,000.

March 1995 – A sarin gas attack on the Tokyo subway killed 12 and injured more than 5,000.

April 1995 – Timothy McVeigh bombed the Federal Building in Oklahoma City, killing 168 and injuring more than 500.

July 1996 – A bomb exploded in Atlanta during the Olympic games, killing one and wounding more than 100. Extreme right wing activist Eric Robert Rudolph was arrested in 2003 and sentenced in 2005.

August 1998 – A car bomb, believed to be planted by the Real IRA, exploded in Omagh, Northern Ireland, killing 29 people and injuring at least 220. Two truck bombs destroyed US Embassies in Kenya and Tanzania, leaving 230 dead.

October 2000 – Suicide bombers, linked to al-Qaeda, attacked the warship USS *Cole*, in Yemen, killing 17 sailors and injuring more than 30.

September 2001 – Two hijacked planes crashed into the World Trade Center, New York City. The Pentagon, in Washington, was struck by a third hijacked plane and a fourth crashed into a field in southern Pennsylvania. In total, over 3,000 lives were lost. Osama bin Laden is considered to be the prime suspect.

November 2001 – The US invaded Afghanistan in search for bin Laden and other al-Qaeda suspects.

December 2001 – Pakistani-backed terrorists attacked the Indian Parliament, killing nine. An American Airlines flight made an emergency landing after a passenger tried to detonate explosives hidden in his shoes. The 'shoe bomber', Richard Reid, was sentenced to life in prison in 2003.

October 2002 – Two car bombs exploded in Bali, killing over 200 people and injuring more than 300 others. Islamic terrorists were held responsible. Chechen rebels stormed a theatre in Moscow and took 800 people hostage. Russian special troops stormed the theatre after a three-day siege but killed over 120 hostages, as well as some of the terrorists.

March 2003 – The US invaded Iraq in their search for supporters of the al-Qaeda network and weapons of mass destruction.

July 2003 – Two female suicide bombers blew themselves up at a rock festival just outside Moscow, killing at least 18 people and injuring more than 50.

February 2004 – A suicide bomb attack on the Moscow underground killed 39 and injured more than 100. Chechen rebels were blamed.

September 2004 – Chechen rebels occupied a school in Russia – 331 children and teachers killed in rescue.

July 2005 – Suicide bombers trained by al-Qaeda blew up three underground trains and a bus in London, killing 53 people.

June 2006 – Abu Musab al-Zarqawi, the leader of al-Qaeda in Iraq, was killed in a US air strike.

July 2006 – Almost 200 people killed in Mumbai, India, train bomb attacks. Hezbollah sent rockets into Israel. Large-scale Israeli bombing of South Lebanon followed.

August 2006 – Plans were discovered to blow up at least 11 airliners flying from the UK to USA. Suspected al-Qaeda members arrested.

45

ORGANISATIONS AND GLOSSARY

African National Congress (ANC)
The ANC was formed in 1912 when tribal chiefs joined together with community and church organisations to defend the rights and freedoms of black people in South Africa.

Al-Jihad
An Egyptian Islamic extremist group who aim to overthrow the Egyptian government and replace it with an Islamic state. Al-Jihad merged with al-Qaeda in 2001, although the group are still capable of independent operations. Also known as Islamic Jihad.

Al-Qaeda
A terrorist organisation devoted to uniting all Muslims and establishing an international, strict Islamic state. The group, led by Osama bin Laden, are suspected of some of the major international terrorist atrocities of the 21st century, including the September 11th attacks in the US and the Bali bomb of 2002.

Aum Shinrikyo (Supreme truth)
The Japanese cult responsible for the Tokyo subway attack in 1995, which killed 12 and injured more than 5,000. Members of the cult believe that the end of the world is near.

Basque Fatherland and Liberty (ETA)
Formed in 1959, the ETA are dedicated to achieving independence for the Basque region of north-western Spain. The group targets police officers, soldiers, government officials and the tourist industry.

Chechen rebels
Terrorists from Chechnya who are fighting for political independence from Russia. The rebels have been blamed for a number of suicide attacks since the 1990s.

Hamas (Islamic Resistance Movement)
An Islamic group formed in 1988. Hamas are fighting for an independent Palestinian state ruled under Islamic law and are responsible for many suicide attacks against Israelis.

Harak ul-Mujahideen (HUM)
A group who aim to establish Islamic rule in Pakistan and Kashmir. HUM has carried out a number of attacks against Indian troops and civilian targets in Kashmir.

Hezbollah (Party of God)
A radical Islamic group from Lebanon. The group seeks a republic that excludes all non-Islamic people.

Irish Republican Army (IRA)
The largest of the Republican terrorist groups that campaigned for a united Ireland for much of the late 20th century. The IRA has many splinter groups such as the Real IRA, the Continuity IRA, the Provisional IRA and the Irish National Liberation Army (INLA).

Islamic Group (IG)
An Egyptian group who seek to overthrow the Egyptian government and replace it with an Islamic state. IG has also been involved in attacks against US interests, such as the 1993 bombing of the World Trade Center. The group is believed to have links with al-Qaeda.

Jemaah Islamiah (JI)
A South-East Asian Islamic fundamentalist group dedicated to the establishment of an Islamic state in Indonesia. Jemaah Islamiah were responsible for the Bali bomb in 2002. The group has links with al-Qaeda.

Kurdistan Workers Party (PKK)
Founded in 1974, the PKK's goal is to establish an independent Kurdish state in south-eastern Turkey, where the population is predominantly Kurdish.

Liberation Tigers of Tamil (LTTE)
The LTTE was formed in the 1970s from economically deprived workers and youth in Sri Lanka. The group seeks an independent state in areas of Sri Lanka inhabited by ethnic Tamils. Also known as the Tamil Tigers.

Muslim Brotherhood
Formed as a peaceful group in Egypt in the 1920s, the Muslim Brotherhood gradually became more aggressive in the 1930s and 1940s. The group seeks social and moral reform based upon Islam.

National Liberation Army (ELN)
A communist group formed in 1965. The ELN has attacked many capitalist targets in Colombia, such as the petroleum industry and foreigners working for large corporations.

Palestine Islamic Jihad (PIJ)
The PIJ is committed to the creation of an Islamic Palestinian state and the destruction of Israel through holy war.

Palestine Liberation Organisation (PLO)
The PLO, formed in 1964, fight for the territorial rights of Palestinians. The group are accused of supporting terrorism although they define themselves as a liberation movement.

Popular Front for the Liberation of Palestine (PFLP)
The PFLP, founded in 1967, regards the Palestinian struggle as a legitimate fight against illegal occupation. The PFLP is opposed to negotiations with Israel.

Red Army Faction (Baader-Meinhof gang)
A communist terror group operating in Germany. During the 1970s, the group attacked targets in West Germany, which it believed had not adequately confronted its Nazi past.

Revolutionary Armed Forces of Colombia (FARC)
FARC was established in 1964 as the military wing of the Colombian Communist Party. The group now boasts around 18,000 members. FARC has attacked Colombian political, military and economic targets in their long-running war against the state.

Shining Path
An extremist faction of the Peruvian Communist Party. The group has been opposed to the Peruvian government since 1980.

Tupac Amaru Revolutionary Movement (MRTA)
Formed in 1983, the MRTA aims to establish a Marxist regime and to rid Peru of imperialist tendencies, such as US and Japanese influences.

Ulster Volunteer Force (UVF)
The leading terrorist organisation in Northern Ireland that strives for continued political unity with the United Kingdom. Other Unionist groups include the Ulster Defence Association (UDA), the Ulster Freedom Fighters (UFF) and the Loyalist Volunteer Force (LVF).

United Self-Defence Forces of Colombia (AUC)
A right wing group formed when drug lords took over local self-defence groups in Colombia to protect their own interests. The group uses violence to silence all those that speak out against them.

Apartheid – A political system enforced in South Africa during the 20th century in which black people were denied basic freedoms and rights.

Assassination – The murder of an important person, such as a politician, by a surprise attack.

Black and Tans – An armed police force sent to Ireland in 1920 by the British government to suppress revolutionary activity. The name comes from the colour of their uniforms.

Christianity – The religion of Jesus Christ, practised by Christians. The New Testament describes his life, death and resurrection in the 1st century AD.

Cyberterrorism – Terrorism that uses modern technology, particularly computer technology, to commit acts of sabotage.

Democracy – A political system that allows choice and power to be shared amongst all people in a society. Democracy originated from ancient Greek society where people were elected to make political decisions.

Dirty bomb – A bomb used to scatter biological or radioactive chemicals throughout an area.

Federal Bureau of Investigation (FBI) – The investigative branch of the US Justice Department, which aims to combat violent crime and protect the US from foreign intelligence and terrorism.

Freedom fighter – The term sometimes used for a terrorist who uses violent methods to overturn an oppressive and unfair government or political system.

Fundamentalist – The extreme application of any religion. Fundamentalism started in Christianity but it now refers to all religions. Fundamentalists believe in strict and traditional interpretations of religious beliefs.

Geneva Convention – One of a series of international agreements, first made in Geneva in 1864, establishing rules for the humane treatment of prisoners of war and of the sick, the wounded and the dead in battle.

Hijacking – When a terrorist takes charge of an aeroplane, train or boat, against the will of its pilot, driver or captain and passengers.

Hostages – People held against their will. Their captors often make demands in exchange for their release.

Islam – The religion founded by the prophet Mohammad in the 7th century. Islam is the youngest of the three world religions that believe in just one god (the others are Judaism and Christianity). A person who follows Islam is called a Muslim.

Jihad – A Muslim holy war or spiritual struggle.

Judaism – The modern term used to describe the religion practised by Jews. The term Jew derives from descendents of Judah, the fourth son of Jacob.

Mafia – An international secret organisation, founded in Sicily in the 19th century. The group are involved in many illegal operations, such as drug smuggling, gambling and corruption.

Mujahideen – The Islamic term for somebody who fights in a jihad (a holy war).

Osama bin Laden – The leader and inspiration behind the al-Qaeda network.

Shah – Formerly, a ruler of certain Middle Eastern countries, such as Iran.

Special Air Service (SAS) – A regiment in the British Army specialising in secret operations, such as intelligence-gathering and combating terrorism.

Taliban – The strict fundamentalist Islamic regime that took charge of Afghanistan in 1996. At the time of the 11 September 2001 attacks, the Taliban were believed to be harbouring the al-Qaeda network in Afghanistan.

United Nations (UN) – An international organisation composed of most of the countries of the world. The UN was founded in 1945 to promote peace, security and economic development.

INDEX

Picture Research: Brian Hunter Smart **Photo Credits:** Abbreviations: l-left, r-right, b-bottom, t-top, c-centre, m-middle
Front cover main and back cover t — Bri Rodriguez/FEMA. Front cover ml, 12b, 25mr — Johnny Bivera/US Navy. Front cover c — USMC. Front cover mr — Preston Keres/US Navy. 1 all, 4mr, 6tr, 7mr, 8bl, 11tr, 14ml, 15br, 16tl, 18 both, 19tl, 21tr, 22bl, 23tr, 26bl, 30tr, 33tl, 34tr, 36tr, 40tl, 40br, 41ml — Photodisc. 2bl, 13c, 14tr — FEMA. 2-3b, 43tl — Lisa Borges/US Navy. 3tr, 22tl — Cherie A Thurlby/US Airforce. 4tr — David Salazar/US Navy. 4bl, 36bl — Alan Lewis/CORBIS SYGMA. 5bl, 6c, 30br, 45tr — Andrea Booher/FEMA. 7tl — D Faram/US Navy. 7c — Ted Banks/US Navy. 9tl, 20tr, 27c, 32t, 37tr, 37c, 38tl, 38br — Corel. 9br — Andre Brutman/Israeli Government Press Office. 10br — Ohayon Avi/Israeli Government Press Office. 11bl — David Turnley/CORBIS. 12tr, 35c, 37tl — Corbis. 14br — Ralf-Finn Hestoft/CORBIS. 16bl — Aaron Peterson/US Navy. 17tl — Alek Malhas/US Navy. 17ml — Bryn Colton/Assignments Photographers/CORBIS. 19br — Steve W Kirtley/USMC. 20ml, 41bl — Flat Earth. 21ml — US Navy. 23br — Bettman/CORBIS. 24ml — Gregory K Funk/USMC. 24mr — Arlo K Abrahamson/US Navy. 24bm — Anthony R Blanco/USMC. 26tr, 29tl — Jim Watson/US Navy. 28mr, 45bl — Adam Johnston/US Airforce. 29br — Matthew A Apprendi/USMC. 31tr — PBD. 31br — Shane T McCoy/US Navy. 34bl, 35tr — Peter Turnley/CORBIS. 39tr — M P Shelato/USMC. 39bl, 41tr — Bill Lisbon/USMC. 40tr — Joseph R Chenelly/USMC. 42b — Eric J Tilford. 43r — Matthew Orr/US Navy. 44tr — Nathan Alan Heusdens/USMC. 44bl — Digital Stock.